Influential Women

Cleopatra

Don Nardo

ReferencePoint
Press®

San Diego, CA

© 2016 ReferencePoint Press, Inc.
Printed in the United States

For more information, contact:
ReferencePoint Press, Inc.
PO Box 27779
San Diego, CA 92198
www.ReferencePointPress.com

LIBRARY OF CONGRESS CATALOGING-IN-PUBLICATION DATA

Names: Nardo, Don, 1947-
Title: Cleopatra / by Don Nardo.
Description: San Diego, CA : ReferencePoint Press, Inc., 2016. | Series:
    Influential women | Includes bibliographical references and index.
Identifiers: LCCN 2015026622 (print) | LCCN 2015029388 (ebook) | ISBN
    9781601529480 (hardback) | ISBN 1601529481 (hardback) | ISBN 9781601529497
    (epub)
Subjects: LCSH: Cleopatra, Queen of Egypt, -30 B.C.--Juvenile literature. |
    Egypt--History--332-30 B.C.--Juvenile literature. |
    Queens--Egypt--Biography--Juvenile literature. | Romans--Egypt--Juvenile
    literature.
Classification: LCC DT92.7 .N37 2016 (print) | LCC DT92.7 (ebook) | DDC
    932/.021092--dc23
LC record available at http://lccn.loc.gov/2015026622

Contents

Searching for the Real Cleopatra

"We Romans are the rulers of the greatest and best parts of the world, and yet we find ourselves spurned [scorned] and trampled upon by a woman of Egypt." These words were spoken by Octavian, adopted son of and political successor to the legendary Roman general Julius Caesar. Only twenty-two, Octavian stood before his troops, exhorting them to fight with all the strength they could muster. Within minutes, he said, they must enter a battle that would decide Rome's fate as a nation and empire, perhaps for all times. They must fight for their loved ones and way of life against "this pestilence of a woman."[1]

The woman Octavian spoke of on that momentous day in September 31 BCE was Cleopatra VII, queen of Egypt. A few years before, she had joined forces with Octavian's brother-in-law, the Roman military general Mark Antony. The couple had sailed their war fleet to Actium, in western Greece, to challenge Rome for supremacy in the Mediterranean sphere—which was, at the time, the political and cultural center of the known world.

"Slaves of a Woman"

"This disgraces our fathers," Octavian went on. "Would we not dishonor ourselves, if, after surpassing other nations in valor, we then meekly endured the insults of this rabble, the natives of Alexandria and of Egypt?" Even worse, the young man asserted as passionately as he could, "they are not ruled by a man, but are the slaves of a woman." Indeed, "who would not tear his hair at the sight of Roman soldiers serving as bodyguards of this queen?"[2]

Octavian's disgust at the idea of Romans becoming "slaves of a woman" was partly a reference to Antony's decision to turn his back on Rome and join Cleopatra. But also, it dredged up the revulsion most men of that era felt for women who defied tradition and cultural norms. The common view was that the members of the fairer sex existed strictly to have children, clean the house, and satisfy the desires of men. The roles of men, on the other hand, revolved around ruling home and country and fighting wars.

To Octavian and other Roman males, therefore, Cleopatra was guilty of three heinous offenses. First, she had dared to oppose Rome. Second, she had used her sneaky, wicked tricks to deceive Antony into betraying his country. Much worse, however, was her third supposed crime—that of being a woman who defied and twisted the natural order, in which men ruled and women obeyed. The typical emotional response to Cleopatra's sins was put into words by Octavian's contemporary, the Roman poet Horace. She was a "monstrous queen," Horace snarled, the leader of a "loathsome herd of creatures vile with disease."[3]

> "Who would not tear his hair at the sight of Roman soldiers serving as bodyguards of this queen?"[2]
>
> —Octavian, who would later become Augustus, the first Roman emperor.

Centuries of Mythmaking

Unfortunately for posterity, including modern observers, this highly biased portrayal of Cleopatra long endured. That image—a shady, scheming woman who corrupted good men and threatened to destroy society's natural order—became history's dominant view of who she was. The way this happened is not surprising. After all, Octavian won the great sea battle at Actium, after which Cleopatra and Antony fled back to Egypt and committed suicide. It was then up to the Romans to write the history of recent events, including Cleopatra's rise and fall, in the terms they saw fit.

Thus, when the Romans took over Egypt following Cleopatra's demise, they did not preserve the administrative, legal, and historical documents of her reign. They also destroyed her writings, which some evidence suggests did exist, or else allowed them to rot away. As a result, mean-spirited hearsay about her—much of it engineered

Over the centuries, artists and writers have depicted Cleopatra as many things. In this painting, a nineteenth-century artist envisions the Egyptian queen in a private moment with a servant who helps her dress and style her hair.

by Rome—flourished, and little factual information survived to reveal the real Cleopatra.

Mythmaking of that sort continued over the course of the centuries. The Roman distortions of the famous queen's character created a host of images of her, mostly unflattering, although a few more positive ones developed as well. As one of her modern biographers, Lucy Hughes-Hallett, puts it, Cleopatra has become many people, most of whom contradict one another. First, "she is a sexual glutton" who seduced one Roman nobleman after another. In contrast, "she is a true and tender lover who died for her man." Hughes-Hallett continues, "she is an untrustworthy foreigner whose lasciviousness and cunning are typical of her race. She is a public benefactor, builder of aqueducts and lighthouses. She is a selfish tyrant who tortures slaves for her entertainment. She is as playful as a child."[4]

> "A capable, clear-eyed sovereign, [Cleopatra] knew how to build a fleet, suppress an insurrection, control a currency, alleviate a famine."[5]
>
> —Stacy Schiff, author of Cleopatra: A Life.

Mixing the Real and Imagined

Faced with so many competing images of Cleopatra, modern historians have tried to cut away the historical lies and cultural clutter. What emerges is a more stable, constructive, and realistic woman. The real person who sat on Egypt's throne and fought Octavian at Actium appears to have been an intelligent and talented individual who did have flaws but also possessed many positive traits.

In fact, Cleopatra's latest major biographer, Stacy Schiff, points out that less biased studies of Cleopatra have shown that she was a match for the best male rulers of her day:

A capable, clear-eyed sovereign, she knew how to build a fleet, suppress an insurrection, control a currency, alleviate a famine. An eminent Roman general vouched for her grasp of military affairs. Even at a time when women rulers were no rarity, she stood out, the sole female of the ancient world to rise alone and to play a [notable] role in Western affairs. She was incomparably richer than anyone else in the Mediterranean [world]. And she enjoyed greater prestige than any other woman of her age.[5]

However, even with the more truly historical Cleopatra emerging in recent times, the older and in various ways mythical Cleopatra cannot and should not be ignored. This is because over the centuries she attracted writers and artists of all kinds. Countless poems, plays, paintings, novels, and films have been based on the myths surrounding her. Many of them have become famous and admired. So they will remain cultural treasures, even if they *can* be shown to be inaccurate depictions. Ultimately, that mix of the real and the imagined has proved to be the lasting power of an ancient queen who lived for only thirty-nine years but went on to inspire millions of people in every succeeding generation.

Chapter One

Growing Up in Rome's Shadow

Plenty is known about Cleopatra's adult deeds, thanks to surviving ancient Roman sources. Even so, modern historians must evaluate these works carefully because the Romans disliked her intensely and, being biased, purposely presented her in a bad light. Also, the three main ancient sources of information about her life were penned long after her death. So at least some of what they say is likely hearsay or not to be trusted for other reasons.

For example, Plutarch, a Greek who became a Roman citizen, wrote a biography of Cleopatra's Roman lover Mark Antony that includes a lot of important information about her. But Plutarch was born in around 46 CE, some seventy-six years after Cleopatra's passing in 31 BCE. The other two main ancient sources were even more removed from their subject. Appian, another Romanized Greek, was born in roughly 95 CE and the Roman Dio Cassius in about 161 CE.

Reliable information about Cleopatra's childhood is even harder to come by. Until fairly recently, extremely little physical or literary evidence was known about her before her young adulthood, when she met the legendary Roman military general Julius Caesar. So historians and her other modern biographers were unable to say much with certainty about her childhood. As Egypt's leading archaeologist, Zahi Hawass, puts it, for more than twenty centuries Cleopatra "remained shrouded in the layers of history, revealing just enough to captivate the world's imagination."[6]

Fortunately for posterity, however, the mysteries surrounding Cleopatra are at last starting to be solved. Beginning in the late 1900s, researchers started compiling previously unknown texts, tax records, astrological charts, and other evidence. Even Cleopatra's own handwriting was authenticated only fairly recently. As University of York scholar Joann Fletcher states,

> With the Roman sources now more evenly balanced with Greek and Egyptian evidence, vital clues in archaeological reports from sites now lost can be combined with details of sites which have only recently come to light, including Cleopatra's own palace quarters, [and the details] of daily life as it was lived in the first century BCE are able to add a further rich layer of detail to what is now known about the woman herself.[7]

The Ptolemaic Dynasty

Within that "rich layer of detail" rests Cleopatra's national and family background. This mass of detail also contains Egypt's evolving political situation during her early years and the physical and cultural surroundings in which she grew and learned. Such factors provide crucial clues to the city, palace, living conditions, and personal relationships she experienced when young.

Cleopatra, the seventh royal woman of that name in Egypt's Ptolemaic era, was born in the country's capital city of Alexandria in 69 BCE. The Ptolemaic period had begun in the late 300s BCE with the ascension of her great-great (and several more greats) grandfather, Ptolemy. A Macedonian Greek, he had started out as one the chief lieutenants of Macedonia's renowned king and conqueror Alexander the Great. In 332 BCE, Alexander liberated Egypt after it had endured close to two centuries of Persian rule and subjugation.

The Egyptians did not gain their independence, however. Instead, their land now became part of Alexander's own rapidly expanding realm.

> "Vital clues in archaeological reports from sites now lost can be combined with details of sites which have only recently come to light, including Cleopatra's own palace quarters."[7]
>
> —Cleopatra biographer Joann Fletcher.

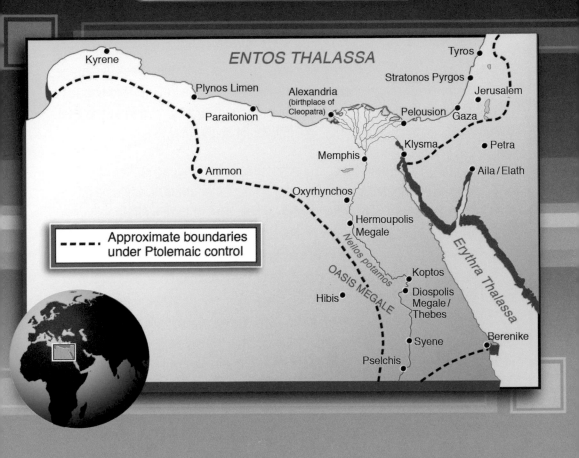

Ptolemaic Egypt c. 270 BC

ENTOS THALASSA

Kyrene
Plynos Limen
Paraitonion
Alexandria (birthplace of Cleopatra)
Ammon
Oxyrhynchos
Memphis
Tyros
Stratonos Pyrgos
Jerusalem
Pelousion
Gaza
Klysma
Petra
Aila / Elath
Hermoupolis Megale
Neilos potamos
OASIS MEGALE
Hibis
Koptos
Diospolis Megale / Thebes
Syene
Pselchis
Berenike
Erythra Thalassa

- - - - Approximate boundaries under Ptolemaic control

Alexander did not linger long in Egypt, because he was eager to head into and conquer Persia's heartland (in what is now Iraq and Iran). But before leaving, he carried out what proved to be an historically significant act. On the Mediterranean coast, east of the Nile River's delta, he established a new Egyptian capital—Alexandria—to replace the old one, Thebes, lying many miles to the south.

Roughly a decade later, in 323 BCE, Alexander died unexpectedly (possibly from alcohol poisoning). By that time he had carved out the biggest empire the world had yet seen. Moreover, he had failed to name a successor. This oversight proved lethal, since his leading generals and governors soon initiated a horribly brutal power

The Language Barrier and Its Biases

Among the many social customs and other cultural aspects that the Macedonian-Greek Ptolemies enforced in Egypt was the Greek language, used exclusively in business and government administration. This linguistic bias is illustrated in the way the Greek tongue developed during the Ptolemaic years. According to the late, influential historian Naphtali Lewis:

> In ordinary cultural contacts, handy words in the language of one group are readily adopted into the language of the other group. It would be difficult, therefore, to exaggerate the significance of the fact that, except for some local designations of places, measures, and so on, no native Egyptian word made its way into Greek usage in the thousand years that Greek endured as the language of Ptolemaic, Roman, and Byzantine Egypt. This phenomenon can only mean that [during the Ptolemaic period] the Greek-speaking population actively resisted using or adopting the Egyptian [language]. In fact, when a need arose, they would exhume and resurrect a Greek term fallen into [disuse] rather than introduce the available Egyptian word into their language and usage.

Naphtali Lewis, *Greeks in Ptolemaic Egypt.* Oxford: Clarendon, 1986, p. 154.

struggle that lasted for more than a generation. In the process, several of those "successors," as people came to call them, founded their own kingdoms.

Ptolemy was one of their number. He seized power in Egypt, where he established a Greek royal dynasty that was destined eventually to produce Cleopatra. Taking the Egyptian title of *pharaoh*, essentially "king," over time Ptolemy expanded the country into an empire. Added were parts of what are now Israel, Syria, and Turkey, along with the large Mediterranean island of Cyprus. Two other important feats, begun by Ptolemy and completed by his son, who ruled as Ptolemy II Philadelphus, were academic in nature. One was the erection in Alexandria of the Museum, a research center that drew the foremost scholars from far and wide. The other achievement was building the world's biggest library, also in the capital.

Ptolemaic Society and Economy

The later Ptolemaic rulers, including Cleopatra's father, King Ptolemy XII Auletes, were absolute monarchs, just as the first two had been. For the average Egyptian, therefore, his or her relationship with the throne was no different than it had been for dozens of centuries. After all, every one of the Egyptian pharaohs and Persian kings had been all-powerful rulers, too.

However, the Ptolemies also established a social system in which most native-born, non-Greek Egyptians were worse off than they had been before the Greek takeover. In this system, which Cleopatra in large degree perpetuated, Greek soldiers, merchants, artisans, and administrators very rarely intermarried or mixed socially with native Egyptians. According to the late American expert on Ptolemaic Egypt, Naphtali Lewis, it "remained throughout its history a land of two cultures that did coexist but, for the most part, did not coalesce, or blend. The families of Greek and Macedonian ancestry, proud of being a 'master race,' saw to that."[8]

> "Throughout its history, [Ptolemaic Egypt was] a land of two cultures that did coexist but, for the most part, did not coalesce, or blend."[8]
>
> —The late classical scholar Naphtali Lewis.

While she was growing up, therefore, Cleopatra was shielded from most everyday aspects of native Egyptian culture. Spending most of her time in the family's palace, she was surrounded by Greek culture and customs. She also conversed with family and friends mostly in Greek, which had long been the lingua franca (universal tongue) of business and government in Egypt.

Indeed, the Ptolemaic government, legal system, and economy were also riddled with that same favoritism for Greeks and their culture. In administration, for instance, Hawass writes, "Greeks held positions of power, while Egyptians were appointed only to low-level positions." At the same time, "there was one set of laws for Egyptians, another for foreigners, and a third for those who lived in

Greek cities within Egypt. Each set of laws had its own set of courts and judges."⁹

Meanwhile, the young Cleopatra observed that her relatives, the elder Ptolemies, also kept tight control over the economy. In part this was to make the money they needed to maintain their fabulous lifestyle—one filled with numerous privileges and luxuries. But those funds were also required to pay the army, which was essential to the family's ability to remain in power. "Agriculture, manufacturing, and trade," Hawass continues, "supported the economy under the Ptolemies. The majority of the agricultural land was controlled by the king and rented to farmers. Temple complexes took up significant amounts of land as well, and Ptolemaic leaders began taking over that land in order to control the power of the priests."¹⁰ Oil, salt, and textiles were important industries. But the most vital of all was papyrus, a kind of paper made from a water plant that grew plentifully along the Nile's banks.

Dependent on Rome's Generosity

There was one overriding and critical political-economic fact that Cleopatra likely did not understand when she was very young. Namely, in spite of her family's military power and efficient control of Egypt's agriculture and other national resources, the kingdom was no longer a key power player on the world's political stage. In fact, it had been so only under the first few Ptolemaic rulers. After that, the dynasty's power and influence had steadily declined until the last few Ptolemies, including Cleopatra's father, were third-rate rulers of a third-rate country.

Part of the reason for this decline was a major shift in the Mediterranean world's balance of power that took place between the mid-200s and late 100s BCE. During those years, Rome, master of the Italian peninsula, swiftly conquered most of the lands bordering the sea, including the Greek city-states and kingdoms lying north of Egypt. The Romans had also imposed their influence over the Ptolemaic realm, the last large-scale independent Greek-ruled state. So by the time of Cleopatra's childhood, Egypt was a client of Rome. That is, the Ptolemies were politically, militarily, and economically dependent on the personal wills and generosity of a few rich and powerful Romans.

Thus, at some point in her upbringing, Cleopatra learned that her country lived always in Rome's mighty shadow and that her father, Ptolemy XII Auletes, spent much of his time begging for money and favors from Roman benefactors. (It remains uncertain who Cleopatra's mother was. Many experts suggest she may have been Auletes's sister, Cleopatra V Tryphaina. The Ptolemies had long before adopted the Egyptian custom of having royal siblings marry.)

One reason that Auletes was frequently indebted to Roman noblemen was that he was a disorganized, ineffective ruler. Not only did he drain the royal treasury through wasteful spending, he also mismanaged the national coinage. For example, to save money he reduced the silver content of coins by two-thirds. This ended up making money worth less, which in turn caused the cost of living to rise sharply. In addition, Auletes raised taxes, hoping to make up for his financial mistakes. But this proved the proverbial last straw for his people, who were driven to the verge of open rebellion by 59 BCE.

A Carefree Life and the Best Possible Education

At this turning point in Auletes's affairs, and the Ptolemaic government's fortunes in general, Cleopatra was ten. Fortunately for her and her royal siblings—two brothers and three sisters—their parents shielded them from the political and economic unrest that was sweeping the country. The children spent many carefree, happy days and years inside the palace, built on the small island of Antirhodos, lying within Alexandria's harbor.

There, young Cleopatra enjoyed a wide array of luxuries, of which the average Egyptian of that era could barely have dreamed. She had on call, day and night, the services of the leading Alexandrian doctors, who were overall the best healers in the known world. She also ate the most appetizing native and imported foods, wore the finest clothes available, and had numerous servants to see to all of her needs.

Cleopatra also had the benefit of the best education available in the entire Mediterranean world. Thanks to the existence of the Museum and Alexandrian Library, erected by the first two Ptolemies, the city had attracted most of the world's most respected scholars. The esteemed local academic community they formed was the pool from which Cleopatra's tutors were drawn.

The full range of subjects she studied as a child and teenager is unknown, but various tidbits of literary evidence provide a rough idea. They included astronomy, possibly taught by the legendary Greek astronomer Sosigenes (who later created the Julian calendar, which remained in use for more than one thousand years); geometry, taught by famous mathematicians who dedicated their books to her; natural history, including the behavior of animals she visited at the royal zoo; and literature. Among the books available to her were the works of the great fifth-century-BCE Athenian playwrights and all the known published history texts, including those by the pioneering Greek historians Herodotus and Thucydides.

> *"Any cultivated Greek, Cleopatra included, could recite some part of [Homer's] Iliad and the Odyssey by heart."[11]*
>
> —Cleopatra's modern biographer Stacy Schiff.

The highlight of Cleopatra's education was undoubtedly her studies of the *Iliad* and *Odyssey*, the monumental epic poems of the eighth-century-BCE Greek bard Homer. Stacy Schiff explains:

No text more thoroughly penetrated Cleopatra's world. In an age infatuated with history [and military] glory, Homer's work was the Bible of the day. He was the prince of literature. His 15,693 lines provided the moral, political, historical, and religious context, the great deeds and the ruling principles, the intellectual atlas and moral compass [for the age]. The educated person cited him, paraphrased him, alluded to him. [Moreover] any cultivated Greek, Cleopatra included, could recite some part of the *Iliad* and the *Odyssey* by heart.[11]

Another aspect of Cleopatra's education, which surely helped shape the worldly character she later displayed, apparently came from *outside* the palace walls. At the time, Alexandria was the most cosmopolitan, or international, city in the Mediterranean sphere. Besides its native Egyptian neighborhoods, it had extensive Greek quarters, as well as a fairly large Jewish sector. In addition, traders, sailors, and tourists from Syria, Arabia, North Africa, and even Ethiopia (lying well south of Egypt) paid regular visits to Alexandria's port district. The result was a veritable melting pot of cultures and languages. That Cleopatra was aware of and impressed by this mix of peoples is proved by the fact that she learned to speak fluent Arabic, Hebrew, and Syriac (a common ancient Middle Eastern language), along with Greek and Egyptian.

Soldiers prepare to descend from the Trojan horse in a sixteenth-century depiction of the scene described in Book 4 of Homer's epic poem, the **Odyssey.** *Cleopatra's education likely included extensive readings of both the* **Iliad** *and the* **Odyssey.**

Auletes Seeks Aid

Cleopatra's fantastic ability to absorb knowledge was bound to pay off for her. Indeed, King Auletes seems to have recognized that she was, from an early age, the most learned, talented, and impressive of all his offspring. Perhaps that is why he decided to introduce her to the nation's political and financial woes when she was only eleven.

At that point, in 58 BCE, Auletes saw that his subjects were becoming dangerously restless over his tax policies and might rebel at any moment. So he sailed to Italy, hoping to obtain the political and military backing and protection of one or more rich and powerful Romans. It is revealing that he took his favorite child, Cleopatra, with him, maybe to expose her to the political wheeling and dealing she would likely encounter herself if she succeeded him on the throne at some future date.

Not long before heading for Rome, Auletes had managed to get an appointment with the up-and-coming Roman politician Julius Caesar. He actually wanted to back Auletes, almost certainly in order to acquire an inroad into Egyptian politics, which he hoped to exploit later. But Caesar was then short of cash, as well as on his way to conquer Gaul (now France), and offered no help.

While in Rome, Auletes learned that another of his daughters, Berenike IV, had seized the Ptolemaic throne in his absence. Now desperate to get the help he needed to overthrow her, he intently lobbied several other Roman senators and military generals. But after many months of meetings, the Egyptian king received no bites.

Next, therefore, the determined Auletes, with young Cleopatra still at his side, traveled eastward to Ephesus, an important Greek city on the Aegean coast of Anatolia (now Turkey). There he finally got the money he sought. The recently appointed Roman governor of Syria, Aulus Gabinius, agreed to put him back on Egypt's throne for the sum of ten thousand talents, equivalent to tens of millions of dollars in modern money. Gabinius's cavalry commander at the time was twenty-eight-year-old Mark Antony. This meeting marked the first encounter between Antony and Cleopatra. The two could not have guessed that they would one day be lovers, have children together, and boldly challenge the might of Rome.

Auletes and Cleopatra accompanied Antony, who led Gabinius's troops southward through Syria, down the Mediterranean coast, and

Ptolemy XII Auletes, a weak king, was beholden to Rome for money and favors. He nevertheless doted on his daughter, taking her with him to Rome and elsewhere, perhaps to teach her the skills needed for one day ruling Egypt.

into Egypt. As they expected, the Roman soldiers easily defeated the disorganized forces mustered by the inexperienced Berenike and her supporters. Once reinstalled as king, Auletes executed Berenike and her lieutenants. When Antony departed, he left a contingent of Gabinius's troops behind to protect Auletes, who was by now hated by just about everybody in his country except Cleopatra.

In Line to Become Queen

Although the last Ptolemaic king tried to rebuild his image with his people and restore his nation's now badly tarnished reputation, these efforts were largely in vain. Auletes died only a few years later, in 51 BCE. Not only had he largely failed as a leader, he also left behind a thorny political mess for his remaining children to sort out. Cleopatra, then about eighteen, was technically next in line for the throne. But for reasons now unknown, Auletes had demanded in his will that she must share power with her ten-year-old brother, Ptolemy XIII.

Cleopatra's Palace Discovered

When growing up, Cleopatra and her siblings spent a great deal of time in the Ptolemaic royal palace, located on Antirhodos Island in Alexandria's wide bay. The island and its royal treasures are no longer visible from the shore because they sank beneath the waves during a massive earthquake in the 700s CE. Soon after that, the island's exact location was forgotten. In 1996, however, after two decades of searching, noted French underwater archaeologist Franck Goddio found Antirhodos, along with numerous artifacts relating to Cleopatra, her Ptolemaic relatives, and everyday Egyptian life. In a 2010 interview published in *Scientific American*, Goddio explained that "Antirhodos is a very small island measuring 300 meters long, by 50 meters wide, so you cannot miss much of it. [On it], we found the foundation of a very big palace. And we knew [from ancient writings that] there was a palace there." What the archaeologists did not initially know was that on another side of the island rested another large building, which turned out to be a temple to the Egyptian mother goddess Isis. This made sense, Goddio said, because Cleopatra was a major supporter of that deity. Other findings included coins; a statue of Auletes, Cleopatra's father; a carved head of Cleopatra's son, Caesarion; and various objects from Alexandrian daily life.

Quoted in Steve Mirsky, "Cleopatra's Alexandria Treasures," *Scientific American*, January 31, 2010. www.scientificamerican.com.

Just as Cleopatra feared might happen, nearly immediately a petty rivalry with the boy began. This unpleasantness was engineered by young Ptolemy's chief advisor, Pothinus, a strong figure in the royal court. Probably to advance his own ambitions, Pothinus, who hated Cleopatra, proceeded to denounce her to the Egyptian army generals. What happened next is unclear. But by September 49 BCE Cleopatra no longer felt safe in the city and fled to Syria.

Wasting no time, the spirited, self-exiled princess started raising her own troops to fight for the throne she felt was rightfully hers. At that point, she had no way of knowing that one of the few friends her father had made in Rome was about to arrive in Egypt. Also unbeknownst to her, the alliance she would forge with that Roman notable was destined to forever change her life. Furthermore, their romantic interlude would become so memorable that people around the globe would still talk and write about it more than twenty centuries after her death.

Chapter Two

Securing Powerful Allies

Having been threatened with prison or death by her younger brother, Ptolemy XIII, and his power-hungry advisor, Pothinus, in 48 BCE, Cleopatra found herself in Syria. There she started hiring mercenaries, soldiers who work strictly for pay. Promising to pay them well after they put her on Egypt's throne, she marched them southward into Egypt and made camp not far from the capital, Alexandria.

At about that same time, several Roman ships approached Alexandria's harbor. The man in charge of this expedition was Julius Caesar, whom Cleopatra's father had approached for money and protection a decade before. Caesar, now involved in a bloody Roman civil war, had just beaten his main rival, Pompey, in Greece. The defeated general had quickly fled to Egypt, in part because he, too, had once negotiated with Auletes. Hopefully, Pompey reasoned, he would find a friendly refuge in the Ptolemaic royal court.

Pompey's hopes were soon dashed, however. By messenger, the boy-king and his shifty advisor told Pompey he was welcome and invited him ashore. But in truth, this was a ruse, as they worried that if they helped the desperate Roman leader, the man who had defeated him, Caesar, would punish them. So they decided to do away with Pompey, assuming this would please Caesar and get him firmly on their side. Betrayed, the unfortunate Pompey was beheaded by assassins disguised as friends as his rowboat neared the Egyptian shore.

As Caesar approached that same shore shortly afterward with a small contingent of troops, he was not yet aware of his rival's untimely demise. But Caesar was well aware of the present political situation in Egypt, including Cleopatra's flight to Syria and return with soldiers, factors he planned to fully exploit to his advantage. In the journal he kept, he described the current situation, saying, "As it happened, King Ptolemy, who was only a boy, was there at the head of a large force, at war with his sister Cleopatra, whom he had ejected from the kingdom a few months beforehand, [and] Cleopatra's camp was no great distance from his."[12]

Caesar Lands in Alexandria

At the time that Caesar wrote those words, he had no way of knowing that he and young Cleopatra, whom he may have briefly met years before in Rome, would become allies and much more. For the moment, he wanted only two things in Egypt. First, he planned to take Pompey into custody. Second, he hoped to establish a strong power base in that land, securing its vast riches and food supplies to back his bid for ultimate power in the Roman world.

Right after landing in Alexandria, Caesar learned that his first goal was impossible and that his second one would be much harder to attain than he had figured. He later recalled:

> At Alexandria I learned of Pompey's death and there, as soon as I disembarked, I heard the shout raised by the soldiers the king [Ptolemy XIII] had left to garrison the town, and saw them running to meet me, because the [fasces, symbols of Roman power] were being carried in front of me. The body of the population all declared that [my arrival] constituted treason against the king. This disorder was brought under control, but for a period of days the crowd continued to assemble and provoke frequent disturbances, and a number of [Roman] soldiers were killed in the streets of the city. In light of this situation, I ordered other legions, which I had formed from Pompey's [defeated] soldiers, to be brought from Asia.[13]

While awaiting his reinforcements, Caesar met with the boy-king and Pothinus. Thinking they would be rewarded for their actions on his behalf, they presented him with his dead rival's detached head. Instead of being pleased, Caesar was appalled at such brutal treatment of a Roman nobleman. Moreover, he was insulted and angered by the disrespectful way he himself was treated. In the words of his primary ancient biographer, Plutarch, "Pothinus made himself intolerable, he littling and insulting Caesar both in his words and his actions. For instance, the soldiers were given rations of the oldest and worst possible grain, and Pothinus told them that they must put up with it and learn to like it, since they were eating food that did not belong to them."[14]

Angry, Caesar now demanded that the Egyptian rulers pay him an enormous sum of money for the support of his army. Further, he said, he would remain in Alexandria for as long as it took to collect those

Julius Caesar is presented with the severed head of Pompey, his rival. Appalled that Ptolemy XIII had treated a Roman nobleman this way, Caesar allied himself with Cleopatra—the boy-king's sister and main rival for the throne.

funds. Considering the poor reception he had received from the boy-king and his advisor, Caesar now saw the wisdom of trying to form some sort of alliance with their chief rival for the throne, Ptolemy's older sister. According to Plutarch, Caesar "secretly sent for Cleopatra from the country."[15]

A Powerful Alliance

Most modern historians feel sure that when Cleopatra got word that Caesar had arrived in the capital, she immediately made plans to secretly contact and welcome him. Although this cannot be known for certain, it does fit her character. She was politically shrewd, even for one so young, and must have realized that his support of her bid for Egypt's throne would be priceless.

Exactly how these two historical titans first met will likely never be known. Plutarch offered an account that sounds too much like a romantic fairy tale to be believed outright, although it is possible that at least some parts of it are based on fact. In that now world-famous story, the would-be queen summoned her servant and friend, Apollodorus the Sicilian. He secretly rowed the two of them under cover of darkness to one side of the royal palace in Alexandria. Plutarch continues:

> "As [Caesar] grew to know [Cleopatra] better, he was overcome by her charm."[16]
>
> —Caesar's ancient biographer Plutarch.

> Since there seemed to be no other way of getting in, she stretched herself out at full length inside a sleeping bag, and Apollodorus, after tying up the bag, carried it indoors to Caesar. This little trick of Cleopatra's, which showed her provocative impudence, is said to have been the first thing about her which captivated Caesar, and as he grew to know her better, he was overcome by her charm.[16]

If this incident actually happened, or if Cleopatra and Caesar met in some other manner, a few crucial facts are more certain. At the time, she was twenty-one and he was fifty-two. Also, he was the most

A Diverse Makeup of Soldiers

While Caesar and Cleopatra were coexisting with her younger brother Ptolemy XIII in the royal palace in Alexandria, the Egyptian military commander Achillas surrounded the structure with portions of his army. This excerpt from the diary-like journal Caesar kept during wartime contains a description of the diverse makeup of the forces that then threatened him and the young would-be queen.

> Achillas was accompanied by forces of a sort not to be despised, either in quantity and type of troops or in military experience. He had 20,000 men under arms. These consisted of Gabinius's soldiers [the Roman troops who had earlier put Cleopatra's father back on his throne], who had by now become habituated to the ill-disciplined ways of Alexandrian life and had unlearned the good name and orderly conduct of Romans and had taken wives, by whom most of them had children. In addition to these, there were men gathered from among the pirates and brigands of Syria, the Cilician province [in southern Anatolia], and adjoining regions. Also, many exiles and men condemned to loss of citizen rights had collected here. All runaway slaves of ours had a guaranteed refuge and a guaranteed way of live at Alexandria, provided they enrolled and became soldiers.

Julius Caesar, *The Alexandrian War,* in *Caesar: The Civil War,* trans. John Carter. New York: Oxford University Press, 1997, p. 137.

powerful man in the known world and strongly desired to assert his political influence in Egypt. Meanwhile, she was anxious to acquire Egypt's throne and urgently needed his backing in her contest with her younger brother. Therefore, Cleopatra and Caesar would each benefit significantly from a mutual pact at that moment in time. As it happened, they not only joined forces politically speaking, but also became personal friends and lovers.

This powerful alliance was totally unexpected by nearly everyone. Indeed, Ptolemy and Pothinus were startled when Caesar suddenly informed them that he was supporting the young woman's claims to Egypt's throne. The terms of Auletes's will must be honored, he told them. Whether they liked it or not, they must let Cleopatra rule jointly with the boy-king, Ptolemy.

At first, Ptolemy and Pothinus agreed to uphold Auletes's will. This was only a political ploy designed to buy time, however, since Pothinus fully intended to get rid of both Caesar and Cleopatra. The ambitious royal advisor secretly sent a message to Achillas, head of Egypt's military, ordering him to bring thousands of soldiers and surround the palace.

What followed was an exceedingly unusual physical and political standoff. For their part, Caesar and Cleopatra were protected by his small company of well-armed bodyguards, yet they were also trapped in the royal palace. At the same time, Ptolemy and Pothinus were trapped there, too, because Caesar stationed some of his guards around them. Thus, the opposing leaders in an escalating conflict lived under the same roof for close to two months while Caesar awaited the arrival of the reinforcements he had sent for earlier.

Cleopatra in Rome

When the end of the strange standoff finally came, events moved swiftly. As soon as word arrived that Caesar's relief force was nearing Alexandria, he had Pothinus killed. Then the newly arrived Romans almost effortlessly defeated Achillas's poorly trained forces outside the city. During the chaotic aftermath of the battle, young Ptolemy fled and then drowned when his overloaded boat sank.

With her rivals out of the way, Cleopatra was now free to ascend the throne as Cleopatra VII. To show how grateful she was for Caesar's help, she took him on a leisurely cruise along the Nile, and they enjoyed a sort of vacation together for the next few months. Finally, however, he informed her that he needed to leave Egypt. The Roman civil war and an insurrection in Anatolia required his attention. It is unknown whether Caesar knew when he departed in 47 BCE that the young queen was carrying his child.

Caesar joins the newly crowned queen of Egypt on a months-long Nile river cruise. By the time the two parted company, Cleopatra was already carrying the Roman leader's child.

The exact date of the child's birth has been lost in the mists of time. More certain is that Cleopatra took the little boy, named Caesarion in honor of his father, with her when she sailed to Rome a little more than a year later, in 46 BCE. By this time the civil war was over, and Caesar was firmly established as Rome's leading military and political leader. He settled her, the child, and their many servants in his beautiful villa situated near the bank of the Tiber River, which flows directly through Rome. There she almost certainly dined and conversed with Caesar's closest associates. Among them was Mark Antony, whom she had met years earlier. By this time, Antony was in many ways Caesar's right-hand man.

It is unclear exactly how long Cleopatra spent in Rome. Some evidence suggests that she returned to Egypt for a while in 45 BCE, but if so, she returned to Rome not long afterward. She was still staying in Caesar's villa when one of history's great turning points occurred. In February 44 BCE, Caesar declared himself dictator for life over Rome and its far-flung realm. He was by all accounts a benign dictator who planned all sorts of building projects and other improvements. But his political enemies would have none of it. A group of senators conspired against him, and on March 15, the Ides of March of that year, they stabbed him to death.

For Cleopatra, alone with her young son and servants across the river, the news of the murder brought shock, grief, and utter fear. For her, Stacy Schiff explains,

> *"Caesar's death represented a catastrophic political blow. [Cleopatra] had lost her champion."[17]*
>
> —Cleopatra's modern biographer Stacy Schiff.

Caesar's death represented a catastrophic political blow. She had lost her champion. Her situation was now insecure at best. The anxiety was great. Were his friends and relatives also to be murdered? Certainly Mark Antony—by rank the next in command—assumed so. Disguised as a servant, he went into hiding. When he resurfaced, it was with a breastplate under his tunic.[17]

Slicing the Territorial Pie

For a while after Caesar's death, Cleopatra kept a low profile in Rome; she hoped to avoid the confusion and hostility on all sides. Later, in early summer, she packed up her belongings, gathered up her young son, and sailed for Alexandria. They reached the city in July 44 BCE.

Once more secure in her palace, Cleopatra watched with interest as the Roman-controlled world shuddered and heaved. Caesar's passing had left behind a major leadership vacuum. Three men sought to fill that political void. To no one's surprise, Mark Antony was one of these men. Also hoping to take advantage of the situation was Caesar's eighteen-year-old adopted son, Octavian. In addition, a popular general named Marcus Lepidus, who had served Caesar loyally, entered the competition.

Cleopatra did not have to wait long to see how the new power struggle would play out. The three rivals decided it would be best not to waste soldiers and resources fighting one another. So they formed an alliance, a three-way power-sharing arrangement that came to be called the Second Triumvirate. In 42 BCE Cleopatra received word that the triumvirs had divided up the Roman world among themselves. Lepidus got the Roman provinces of North Africa, and Octavian received Spain and the large island of Sardinia (off Italy's western coast), as well as Italy.

It was Antony who ended up with the most valuable slices of the territorial pie, however. He took charge of what the Romans called the "East," consisting of the populous and economically successful Roman provinces in Greece, Anatolia, and the Middle East. This gave him a great deal of influence over several weak independent eastern kingdoms, including Egypt. With such potent authority, including command of tens of thousands of Roman troops, Antony decided to pursue an exploit that would bring him much prestige and glory. He began planning an invasion of Parthia, occupying what is now Iraq and Iran—essentially the core of the old Persian Empire.

> "There was an attraction in [Cleopatra's] person and her talk, together with a peculiar force of character which pervaded her every word and action and laid all who were associated with her under her spell."[18]
>
> —Caesar's ancient biographer Plutarch.

Antony Her New Ally?

For that large-scale military adventure, Antony required many ships and soldiers, immense amounts of grain and other foodstuffs, and a lot of money. Parts of the eastern Mediterranean region had varying amounts of these things. But Egypt had all of them in abundance, especially grain. So Antony contacted Cleopatra late in the summer of

Cleopatra's Grand Entry

In a now famous passage from his biography of Antony, Plutarch recalls the Egyptian queen's spectacular arrival in the harbor at Tarsus in 41 BCE, a scene destined to be recreated in countless paintings, novels, and films.

> She came sailing up the river Cydnus in a barge with a stern of gold, its purple sails billowing in the wind, while her rowers caressed the water with oars of silver, which dipped in time to the music of the flute, accompanied by pipes and lutes. Cleopatra herself reclined beneath a canopy of gold cloth, dressed as Venus [Roman goddess of love], while on either side [of her] stood boys costumed as Cupids, who cooled her with fans. Instead of a crew, her barge was lined with the most beautiful of her waiting-women attired as [minor goddesses], some at the rudders, others at the tackle [rigging] of the sails, and all the while [the scent of] an indescribably rich perfume [drifted] from the vessel to the river-banks. [Masses of people] hurried down from the city of Tarsus to gaze at the sight.

Plutarch, *Life of Antony,* in *Makers of Rome: Nine Lives by Plutarch,* trans. Ian Scott-Kilvert. New York: Penguin, 2004, p. 293.

41 BCE and asked her to meet him at his headquarters at Tarsus, in southern Anatolia.

There the two met, discussed business, and began to form a romantic relationship. Antony was unable to resist her charms, which were, according to Plutarch, "irresistible." Furthermore, he wrote, "There was an attraction in her person and her talk, together with a peculiar force of character which pervaded her every word and action and laid all who were associated with her under her spell. It was a delight merely to hear the sound of her voice, with which, like an instrument of many strings, she could pass [effortlessly] from one language to another."[18]

The Roman general Mark Antony and Egypt's Queen Cleopatra meet in 41 BCE in Anatolia. The two felt an immediate attraction, which led to their legendary love affair.

The meeting was fruitful in other ways as well. Cleopatra agreed to back Antony's Parthian expedition, and in exchange he promised to protect her against any enemies who might threaten her nation in the future. Clearly, with Caesar dead, she needed to find another powerful ally, and Antony appeared to be the best possible candidate. Because his Parthian invasion was not scheduled to launch until the following spring (of 40 BCE), she invited him to spend the winter in Alexandria, and he accepted.

Antony was already a married man, whose wife, Fulvia, lived in Rome. But that did not stop him from carrying on an affair with Cleopatra; the two enjoyed many expensive parties, feasts, dice games, and side trips in her luxurious river barges. Eventually, however, reality intruded into the lovers' private little world. Early in 40 BCE, news came that Fulvia, and Antony's younger brother, Lucius, had led an uprising against Octavian back in Italy. Their goal had been to break up the triumvirate, eliminate Octavian, and thereby afford Antony more land and power than he already had. The worst news was that the rebellion had failed. Lucius had been thrown into prison, and Fulvia had fled to Greece.

Hearing this disturbing account, Antony was, in Plutarch's words, "like a man who had been roughly awoken after sleeping off a heavy debauch [drunken stupor]."[19] Quickly, he prepared to sail to Greece to meet with Fulvia. Cleopatra was likely already in love with him, but she was also a queen and a political realist. She knew he had to deal with his headstrong wife and the trouble she had caused with Octavian and the triumvirate.

Still, Cleopatra was now pregnant with Antony's child. It was only natural for her to fret that he might not return to Egypt, in which case the new baby might never have the chance to meet his or her father. After Antony's departure, Cleopatra recognized it would be impossible not to worry about him. But she decided to try to concentrate most of her energies on the roles of motherhood and ruling queen of Egypt. She was about to prove herself extremely effective at both jobs.

Chapter Three

Proving Herself an Effective Ruler

During the roughly three-year-long period following Antony's departure from Egypt in 40 BCE, Cleopatra did not see him at all. Nor did she meet with any other high-placed Romans. Instead, she devoted the vast bulk of her time and energy to running her country.

Very little of a specific nature is now known about her domestic acts and policies during the years she oversaw Egypt alone. In part, this is because most ancient writers did not view the day-to-day mechanics of government administration as important enough to record for posterity. Another reason for the missing details of her reign is that almost all the political documents she signed have not survived.

Nevertheless, the handful of reliable facts about Cleopatra's reign show that she was a well-organized, disciplined, and overall capable leader. In particular, it appears that she managed the economy well and in general treated her people fairly and justly. Tax collection occurred without major protests, and no known rebellions marred her reign.

Part of what made Cleopatra an effective ruler, modern historians believe, was a desire to prove that she could run a nation as well as, or even better than, a man could. She was undoubtedly a smart, alert, and thoughtful individual. She was also tough and resourceful, and she seems to have learned to apply those strengths to ruling her people. That made her an unexpected force to be reckoned with in what was, in regards to leaders of countries, decidedly a man's world.

Toward an Efficient Economy

Cleopatra seems to have sensed that she could not be an efficient ruler unless she found ways to maintain a strong economy. Here she had an advantage that other nations, including the mighty Rome, lacked. Although Egypt had lost much standing in the power politics of the Mediterranean world in recent times, the earlier Ptolemies had had one major policy to their credit. Namely, they had created and sustained the closest thing to a planned economy as existed in those times.

The typical ancient approach to economics on a national scale was to maintain the same agricultural and other commercial practices as one's ancestors had. No significant attempts were made to organize large numbers of farmers, laborers, or other workers to increase efficiency. One noted exception had occurred some twenty-five centuries before Cleopatra's birth, when a few early Egyptian pharaohs had managed to create the labor forces needed to erect the great pyramids. They called on thousands of farmers, who were in the downtime between planting and harvest, to temporarily work as construction laborers.

In a similar manner, several of Cleopatra's Greek predecessors on Egypt's throne attempted to organize large numbers of farmers and other workers. Their goal was to maximize the production of crops and other economic goods. For example, they divided land according to levels of productivity. The most fertile fields were rented out to farmers, who had to follow strict rules for how and when they planted and harvested their crops. Government inspectors kept a close eye on how much grain grew in specific fields. They then told local farmers how much of their harvests should be given to the state as a kind of rental fee for using that land. In the case of less-productive lands, the rules were less strict. Overall, this system, though far from perfect, gave the royal palace a rough but fairly realistic idea of how much food the country would produce in a given season.

Cleopatra followed this same plan for growing grains, fruits, and vegetables, counting on advisors and inspectors to help her keep things running smoothly. Her administration also tightly oversaw the production of other important goods. Among them were the oils pressed from olives, sesame seeds, linseeds, and safflower; textiles made from wool, linen, and hemp; salt; and beer.

Dealing with National Crises

Like rulers across the world, Cleopatra was able to achieve success in economic areas, especially agriculture, only when nature cooperated with her efforts. The first-century-CE Roman philosopher and playwright Seneca the Younger recalled, "It is well established that in the reign of Cleopatra the Nile did not flood for two successive years, the tenth and eleventh of her reign."[20] Historians have calculated that the two years in question were 42 and 41 BCE.

The flood to which Seneca referred, which the Egyptians called "the inundation," was both gentle and essential to raising crops in Egypt. Each year, like clockwork, the Nile slowly crept over its banks and delivered up to a foot or more of fresh water to farmers' fields. When the inundation was smaller than normal or did not come at all, a serious crisis was at hand. Crops might fail, and many people might starve. Without food, the population might also become more susceptible to diseases of various kinds.

Egypt's farmers have always depended on the annual flooding of the Nile River (pictured in more recent times) for irrigating their crops. Flooding did not occur during part of Cleopatra's reign, a situation that would have strained efforts to feed the population.

Exactly how Cleopatra dealt with the water emergencies of 42 and 41 BCE is uncertain. But most scholars think it was similar to what she had done the year before, in 43 BCE. What Seneca did not report was that in that year, although the Nile's waters did not entirely fail to flood, they did fall short of the amount needed to irrigate Egypt's fields. As a result, the amount of grain harvested was not enough to feed everyone.

Evidence suggests that Cleopatra reacted to this crisis by implementing wise and effective moves. First, she ordered that some of the vast amounts of reserve grain stored in Alexandria's royal warehouses be distributed to needy families in the Nile Delta region. Second, she ordered her trusty chief administrator Kallimachos to institute similar anti-famine measures farther to the south, in the region of the old capital, Thebes. His efforts were so successful that as a token of thanks the residents of the area erected statues of him.

When the water crisis worsened, in 42 and 41 BCE, it appears that Cleopatra did her best to deal with the consequences. She almost surely released more grain from the royal storehouses. Also, when outbreaks of sickness occurred, she called on her medical advisor, Dioscurides Phakas, to step in and help. He conducted research on certain illnesses, particularly bubonic plague. Exactly what he discovered about that disease and how he tried to treat it remains unknown because his multivolume medical work did not survive.

Meanwhile, the queen fell back on traditional ways to fight outbreaks of the plague and other sicknesses. As the nation's chief intermediary between humans and the gods, she led public religious ceremonies designed to rid the country of evil. Archaeologists have found stone monuments inscribed with carved scenes of such rituals. In one, a queen, whom experts think is Cleopatra, shakes a large rattle called a sistrum in an effort to appease Sekhmet, the goddess the Egyptians thought sometimes unleashed disease on earthly societies.

The Effective Use of Wealth

In large part because of Cleopatra's sound economic policies, the Egyptian royal treasury, which had shrunk considerably under her father and other earlier Ptolemaic rulers, steadily grew in size. That enabled her to finance large-scale projects of various kinds. One was

Antony's Parthian campaign, to which she donated huge quantities of food, weapons, and other supplies.

In the domestic sphere, Cleopatra initiated several large-scale building projects. The best-known in her day was the creation of the Caesareum, a temple-like structure that stood in the heart of Alexandria. As its name suggests, she built it to honor the memory of her first Roman ally and lover, Caesar. When it was completed in 30 BCE, a lofty granite obelisk stood on each side of the main entrance. Each stood 69 feet (21 m) high and weighed nearly 200 tons (181 metric tons). These impressive obelisks later came to be called "Cleopatra's Needles."

The rest of the Caesareum was no less impressive than the giant pillars that marked its entranceway. According to a surviving description by the ancient writer Philo of Alexandria:

> "The floors of [Cleopatra's] dining rooms were strewn with [roses] a cubit deep, in net-like festoons spread over everything."[22]
>
> —The second-century-CE Greek scholar Socrates of Rhodes.

There is elsewhere no sanctuary like that which is called the Caesareum, a temple to Caesar, patron of sailors, situated on a spit of land facing the harbors famed for their excellent moorings, huge and conspicuous, forming an area of vast breadth, embellished with porticoes [roofed walkways], libraries, men's banqueting halls, groves, [splendid gateways], spacious courtyards, open-air rooms, in short everything which lavish expenditure could produce to beautify it. The whole [structure is] a hope of safety to the voyager whether going into or out of the harbor.[21]

The Caesareum was only one of many new buildings that Cleopatra added to the fast-growing city of Alexandria. Their great size and high level of artistic decoration made Egypt seem grander than ever, while also flaunting Cleopatra's personal power and esteem as a ruler. Another way she showed off her royal status and prestige was to throw lavish state dinners for local Greek nobles and visiting foreign dignitaries. The second-century-CE Greek scholar Socrates of Rhodes left behind the following account of one of those feasts, saying:

The service was wholly of gold and jeweled vessels made with exquisite art; even the walls were hung with tapestries woven of gold and silver threads. And having [prepared] twelve triclinia [dining areas], Cleopatra invited [a foreign dignitary] and his chosen friends. [They were] overwhelmed with the richness of the display; but she quietly smiled and said that all these things were [gifts] for [them]. [Each of the guests] was allowed to take away the couch on which he had lain [while eating]. Even the sideboards, as well as the spreads for the couches, were divided among the guests. [For this single banquet] she distributed fees amounting to a talent [the equivalent of almost twenty years' pay to the average worker in those days] for the purchase of roses. And the floors of the dining rooms were strewn with them a cubit [about twenty inches] deep, in net-like festoons spread over everything.[22]

Cleopatra built the Caesareum in Alexandria to honor the memory of Caesar. At the structure's entrance were two immense granite obelisks (one of which still stood when a French artist painted this scene around the late 1700s). The obelisks came to be known as "Cleopatra's Needles."

Cleopatra's Decree on Taxes

One thing that made Cleopatra an effective ruler was that, when unexpected natural events caused economic shortages, she did not overtax her people to make up the shortfall. Evidence for that fact appears in a surviving decree she issued on April 13, 41 BCE, in the midst of that year's major water crisis. The document reads in part:

> Nobody should demand of [the farmers] anything above the essential Royal Dues [standard taxes], [or] attempt to act wrongfully and to include them among those of whom rural and provincial dues, which are not their concern, are exacted. We, being extremely indignant [about overtaxation] and considering it well to issue a General and Universal Ordinance regarding the whole matter, have decreed that all those from the City, who carry on agricultural work in the country, shall not be subjected, as others are, to demands for [gifts and special taxes people were traditionally forced to give the government] such as may be made from time to time. . . . Nor shall any new tax be required of them. But when they have once paid the essential dues, in kind or in cash, for cornland and for vineland, [they] shall not be molested for anything further, on any pretext whatever. Let it be done accordingly, and this [decree] put up in public, according to law.

Gustave Lefebvre, trans., "The Last Decree of the Lagides," *Melanges Holleux*, Paris, France, 1913, pp. 103–105.

Cleopatra's tremendous wealth and frequent effective use of it for both her people and herself demonstrated how far she had come in a fairly short time span. Only a decade before, she had been an exiled young princess frantic to recover her stolen throne. By the early 30s BCE, however, she was quite literally the richest, most powerful woman in the known world. She was also fast on the way to becoming a leading player on the Mediterranean world's political stage.

A Master of Propaganda

Building the strong public image of a major international political figure was no easy task in Cleopatra's time. She was well aware of that fact. But far from being discouraged or intimidated, she viewed it as a challenge. She had closely observed her father's mostly ineffective policies and career as a king, as well as the poor public image he had projected. So she came to see that she must become more than simply a better ruler than he had been. She also had to become a master of propaganda—spreading hand-picked information designed to promote herself, her abilities, and her reign.

Cleopatra was very successful in this effort. Over time she crafted a striking official portrait of herself and her policies and achievements. That portrait had three main dimensions. First, she projected the image of a compassionate mother figure who cared deeply about her people and their welfare. Second, she worked hard to show that a woman could be an effective national ruler. Many people, both inside and outside of Egypt, saw women as inherently weak and lacking the talents required of a ruler. So she set out to prove that she was strong enough both to defend Egypt and to expand its influence.

The third part of Cleopatra's propaganda effort was to show that she possessed a special ability, one that appeared to reinforce the first two aspects of her image. That ability consisted of a supposed personal connection with divine forces. That is, she claimed to have been chosen by the gods, not only to rule Egypt, but also to make the country greater and more powerful than ever before.

Cleopatra turned out to be a gifted propagandist. No doubt her advisors helped in this department. Yet some evidence indicates that she molded much of her public image herself. Furthermore, she succeeded in widely advertising that new persona in the most effective way open to her at the time.

Today, most public figures build up their images through newspapers, magazines, the Internet, and other formats. But in Cleopatra's era most people could not read. So she skillfully manipulated visual images of herself, including those in paintings, stone carvings, and especially her public appearances before large crowds. In the latter case, she used "the language of drama and spectacle," Lucy Hughes-Hallett explains. That language was "designed to enhance her perceived image, to justify her policies, and to further her cause." Indeed, "between the lines of the ancient written accounts of her career one can watch a fantastic pageant being performed, a pageant which is simultaneously a sequence of real events and the symbolic and immensely exaggerated representation of them."[23] Another way of saying it is that Cleopatra often expertly designed and took part in public spectacles that were carefully fashioned to impress and even stun all who witnessed them.

"The Face of a Queen"

Of the public spectacles in which Cleopatra took part, by far the most splendid and effective were the ones in which she equated herself with the country's most popular goddess—Isis. Thought to oversee the growth and harvesting of wheat and other crops, Isis was also routinely depicted as a benevolent mother figure and forgiver of sins. At some time in Cleopatra's reign, when in public she boldly began to mimic the traditionally accepted appearance of Isis. Plutarch wrote that she "wore the [black] robe which is sacred to Isis, and she was addressed [by her subjects] as the New Isis."[24] No one actually thought the queen was Isis. The belief was that the goddess had asked Cleopatra to represent her on earth by portraying her in religious ceremonies.

> *"Between the lines of the ancient written accounts of [Cleopatra's] career one can watch a fantastic pageant being performed."[23]*
>
> —Cleopatra's modern biographer Lucy Hughes-Hallett.

But what about the real Cleopatra—the woman who existed beneath all the hype of her official propaganda? In recent years more and more evidence has emerged to show that the authentic Cleopatra was an extraordinary individual in her own right. Indeed, Plutarch's famous remark that she was a delight to converse with only scratched the surface of her good points. She was smart, talented, charming, and articulate. She also showed herself to be calm, creative, courageous, and effective in a crisis. In addition, her unwavering allegiance to Caesar, and later to Antony, show how loyal and reliable she was.

In looking at Cleopatra as a ruler, modern experts have also tried to determine what she looked like. No surviving ancient texts provide

Ancient Egyptian artwork depicts what is believed to be Cleopatra representing herself as the reincarnation of the goddess Isis. Isis was thought to oversee crop growth and harvests as well as granting forgiveness of sins.

an exact description of her, so historians must turn to artistic and archaeological evidence. For instance, several ancient busts said to depict her now rest in museums around the world. None of these likenesses, however, have yet been widely accepted as genuine by a majority of scholars.

More promising are the images supposedly showing Cleopatra's face on a few surviving coins. Most of these artifacts are too worn to make out fine details, but a handful are in fairly good condition, and they all display subjects having similar physical features. In the words of historian Diana Preston, they "depict a woman with high cheekbones, strong jaw, and even more pronounced nose, whose face looks hawkishly powerful."[25] Another scholar, the late Ernle Bradford, adds, "The eyes, the height of the brow, the clarity of the features, the nose and chin, all suggest a woman of intellect and power." This, he goes on, "is the face of dignity—the face of a queen."[26]

Cleopatra's Cures for Baldness

One of the many talents Cleopatra possessed, according to several ancient accounts, was writing books on varied subjects. One of these volumes was said to be about cosmetics and supposedly contained cures for male baldness. The original book was lost over the centuries, but the ancient Greek physician Galen quoted from it in his own writings, and in that way the baldness cures survived. One states, "For bald patches, powder red sulfur or arsenic and [soak it in] oak gum, as much as it will bear. Put [the resulting paste] on a rag and apply [to the head], having soaped the place well first." Another hair loss cure that Cleopatra supposedly passed along recommended the following ingredients and procedures:

> Of domestic mice burned, 1 part; of vine-rag burned, 1 part; of horse's teeth burned, 1 part; of bear's grease, 1; of deer's marrow, 1, of reed bark, 1. To be pounded when dry, and mixed with lots of honey; then the bear's grease and marrow [should] be mixed, when melted, [and] the medicine [should] be [rubbed onto] the bald part [of the head] till it sprouts [hair].

Quoted in George Bernard Shaw, *Caesar and Cleopatra*. New York: Brentano's, 1906, p. 114.

It was this strong, shrewd queen who ruled Egypt wisely and effectively in the years that Antony was away in Italy. She had proved she could run a country without the help of a man. Yet as subsequent events would reveal, she had grander ambitions, including carving out an empire. For that, she needed the help of a well-connected Roman with access to large armies. That Roman was Antony, whom she was confident would sooner or later return to her. First, she was by far the most captivating woman he had ever met. Second, less than a year after he left Egypt, she had given birth to twins, a boy and a girl—Antony's children. Thus, Cleopatra reasoned, Egypt harbored magnetic attractions for him that would surely lure him back. The only question in her mind was how long she would have to wait.

> *"The eyes, the height of the brow, the clarity of the features, the nose and chin, all suggest a woman of intellect and power."*[26]
>
> —The late scholar Ernle Bradford.

Chapter Four

Challenging the Might of Rome

During the three years that followed Antony's departure from Egypt in early 40 BCE, Cleopatra's spies kept her informed of his activities in Rome. She learned that in October of the following year, he had patched up his rocky relationship with his primary partner in the Second Triumvirate, Octavian. (It was widely recognized that the third triumvir, Lepidus, was the weakest member of the group. Indeed, Octavian and Antony did not even bother to consult him about the resolution of their differences.)

For Cleopatra, the most disturbing piece of news about Antony concerned the manner in which he and Octavian sealed their new friendship pact—officially called the Treaty of Brundisium. Namely, Antony agreed to marry Octavian's sister, Octavia. (Antony's first wife, Fulvia, had recently died in Greece, so he was free to marry again.) Nevertheless, Cleopatra was confident that Antony would return to Egypt in the near future. He needed her help in equipping his upcoming Parthian expedition. And, she reasoned, he would almost certainly want to visit their infant twins, whom she had named Alexander Helios and Cleopatra Selene.

Antony's Real Agenda

The young Egyptian queen's expectations that her Roman ally and lover would reunite with her in the near future proved well founded. In 37 BCE Antony left his new bride, Octavia, behind in Rome and rushed off to Syria to prepare for his long-anticipated attack on Parthia. Almost immediately after landing in the large Syrian port city of Antioch, he sent for Cleopatra. His resumption of an alliance and personal relationship with her was clearly a major betrayal of his wife, Octavia. Moreover, indirectly it put a huge strain on his relationship with his wife's brother and fellow triumvir, Octavian. It was now clear to all that Antony had agreed to the treaty with Octavian and the marriage to Octavia only to buy time before pursuing his real agenda.

In fact, history has shown that Antony was almost certainly positioning himself for a major challenge to Octavian's power base—essentially Italy and Rome's western provinces. Antony was apparently sure of success in such a venture. This is not surprising, since he had control of Rome's eastern provinces and could count on Cleopatra's considerable wealth and resources. These impressive assets gave him the real potential to push Octavian aside and seize control of the entire Mediterranean world.

Antony's confidence that he would ultimately be able to defeat and eliminate Octavian was also based on a mistaken notion that Caesar's great-nephew and adopted son was too young, politically inexperienced, and militarily naive to pose a serious threat. Despite his age (twenty-six in 37 BCE), Octavian was exceedingly shrewd, devious, and ambitious. Proof of this came in September 36 BCE. To the surprise of many people, including Antony and Cleopatra, Octavian suddenly took control of Lepidus's troops and forced him out of the triumvirate and into exile.

Not long after that, Cleopatra and Antony showed that they had not only underestimated Octavian, but also overestimated Antony's military abilities. In that same year—36 BCE—Antony launched his Parthian invasion. Although he commanded a large army, he soon found that he had badly misjudged the long distances his soldiers would need to cover and the ruggedness of the regions in which they would be fighting. As a result, the expedition ended the following year in utter failure.

The Propaganda War

Antony returned to Egypt in 35 BCE to find a full-scale propaganda war in progress. Octavian and his close associate Marcus Agrippa recognized the value of tearing down an opponent's reputation well before any physical fighting began. They knew that in order to succeed in the coming conflict, Cleopatra and Antony needed the backing of several small independent kingdoms in the East. If Octavian could sufficiently blacken his adversaries' names, the theory went, some of those kingdoms might think twice about supporting Egypt's queen and her Roman lover.

Octavian certainly had a good deal of dirt to throw at Antony. One major black mark against him was that he had suddenly abandoned Octavia. She had a reputation for kindness and virtue and was admired across and beyond the Roman realm. In fact, Antony had done worse than merely leave his new bride. At Cleopatra's request, he also divorced her and even committed the mean-spirited act of ordering some of his officers to physically evict her from their house in Rome. Most Romans saw this as unnecessary and cruel, sentiments that aided Octavian's cause.

Octavian also targeted Cleopatra. She was little more than a prostitute, his propaganda campaign asserted, a loose woman who had

Surrounded by luxuries that few could imagine, Cleopatra awaits a visit from her lover Mark Antony. In an effort to destroy Antony and Cleopatra's hold on power, Octavian portrayed the Egyptian queen as using her wiles to bewitch the renowned Roman general.

used deceit and trickery to corrupt the once noble and honest Antony. Not only had she bewitched him, the story went, her scandalous helpers had drugged him. Supposedly their nefarious goal was to keep him in a constant stupor so that they could bend him into betraying his country. Thus, Plutarch later explained, "Antony was no longer responsible for his actions."[27]

Still more propaganda issued by Octavian was based on what his spies in Alexandria had been telling him. They said that Antony had started wearing Egyptian outfits instead of Roman clothes, part of his unhealthy makeover at Cleopatra's hands. The second-century-CE Roman historian Dio Cassius stated that the conniving queen had so totally enslaved Antony that he followed her orders without question. Also, Dio said, "she had Roman soldiers," Antony's own men, "in her bodyguard, all of whom had her name inscribed upon their shields." These realities "gave the impression that she had laid him under some spell and deprived him of his wits. Indeed, she so enchanted and enthralled," or charmed Antony "that she came to entertain the hope that she would rule the Romans as well." Dio quoted her as saying in public, "I shall one day give judgment," or call the shots, "on the Capitol."[28] This was widely understood to be a reference to Rome's sacred Capitoline Hill.

> "Antony was no longer responsible for his actions."[27]
>
> —Caesar's ancient biographer Plutarch.

Chosen by the Gods?

Octavian's unflattering misinformation campaign did at least some damage to its targets' reputations. In response, the lovers countered with propaganda of their own. During this period, their relationship continued to grow; proof of this came in 35 BCE when Cleopatra gave birth to their third child, a boy they named Ptolemy Philadelphus.

The new baby, along with Cleopatra and Antony's other two children, were key to the couple's propaganda efforts against Octavian. This was because those offspring were destined one day to inherit the immense empire their parents hoped to create in the upcoming war. Cleopatra and Antony's approach to the propaganda battle had less to do with blackening Octavian's name and reputation and more to do with inflating their own reputations. Their agents spread the word

The Donations of Alexandria

The large-scale public ceremony known as the Donations of Alexandria, staged in 34 BCE, was Cleopatra and Antony's largest single propaganda effort in the lead-up to the inevitable war with Octavian. In front of thousands of spectators, the couple reaffirmed their own authority as rulers and heaped honors on their children, giving each the future right to rule a large slice of eastern territory. About the lavish event, Plutarch said in part that Antony

> proclaimed his own sons by Cleopatra to be Kings of Kings. To Alexander he gave Armenia, Media, and Parthia, as soon as he should have conquered it, and to Ptolemy [he gave], Phoenicia, Syria, and Cilicia. At the same time he presented his sons to the people, Alexander in a Median costume, which was crowned by a tiara, and Ptolemy, in boots, a short cloak, and a broad-brimmed hat encircled by a diadem [crown]. [Ptolemy] wore Macedonian dress like the kings who succeeded Alexander the Great, and [Alexander wore] the dress of the Medes and Armenians. After the children had embraced their parents, the one was given a guard of honor of Armenians and the other of Macedonians. Cleopatra, not only on this but on other public occasions, wore the robe which is sacred to Isis.

Plutarch, *Life of Antony,* in *Makers of Rome: Nine Lives by Plutarch,* trans. Ian Scott-Kilvert. New York: Penguin, 1965, pp. 321–22.

near and far that the couple had been chosen by the gods to rule the entire world.

A crucial aspect of this effort to glorify Cleopatra, Antony, and their children involved public religious ceremonies in which the family often took part. As she had in the past, Cleopatra continued to portray herself as an earthly manifestation of the goddess Isis. At the same time, when in public, Caesar's son Caesarion dressed and acted as Isis's divine son, Horus. Antony's role, meanwhile, was to identify himself with the mysterious and popular Greek fertility god Dionysus.

Antony did this partly by issuing coins showing himself dressed as Dionysus. He and Cleopatra also erected statues of themselves wearing Dionysus's and Isis's traditional garb.

The biggest single piece of propaganda engineered by Cleopatra and Antony was an enormous public festival and ceremony that came to be called the Donations of Alexandria. Staged in 34 BCE, the spectacular event drew vast crowds of both Egyptians and visitors

Cleopatra and her son by Julius Caesar, Caesarion, can be seen in this ancient Egyptian artwork. In 34 BCE Antony named Cleopatra and Caesarion co-rulers of Egypt, Cyprus, Libya, and Syria.

from neighboring lands. Those foreign visitors were actually the key audience. This was because the main theme of the spectacle was the bold proclamation that Antony, Cleopatra, and their children were not only the great hope of the East against Rome, but also the future leaders of the known world. The climax of the ceremony, Plutarch recalled, consisted of the couple's granting of various eastern lands and territories to the children. Cleopatra and Antony "assembled a great multitude in the athletic arena," of Alexandria, Plutarch wrote. Antony made sure there were "two thrones of gold, one for himself and one for Cleopatra, placed on a dais of silver, with smaller thrones for his children. First, he proclaimed Cleopatra queen of Egypt, Cyprus, Libya, and Syria, and named Caesarion as her consort [companion]."[29]

> "[Antony] proclaimed Cleopatra queen of Egypt, Cyprus, Libya, and Syria."[29]
>
> —Caesar's ancient biographer Plutarch.

Octavian's spies were also in the audience. Not surprisingly, when they returned to Italy and described what they had seen, the main reactions were resentment and anger. Yet it was clear that many Romans in the East had been impressed by the Donations event. Thus, Octavian realized, he had to counter this very effective piece of propaganda. In the year that followed, Plutarch said, Octavian "did his utmost to rouse the Roman people's anger against"[30] Cleopatra and Antony. This effort included spreading more false rumors about them. According to Dio, one of these manufactured stories claimed that Antony was planning to "hand over the city of Rome to Cleopatra and transfer the seat of [Roman] government to Egypt."[31]

Agrippa Seizes the Initiative

This relentless propaganda war continued for two more years. Antony and Cleopatra fared well in the East, while Octavian won public support mainly in Italy and other western Roman regions. Yet not everyone in the West thought that backing Octavian was prudent. The East's population was larger than the West's, which meant that eastern leaders could potentially raise bigger armies. Also, several eastern leaders, including Cleopatra, possessed vast wealth and natural resources. Many prominent western Romans felt this gave her and Antony a real

Antony Enslaved by Cleopatra?

In ancient times it was customary for a general to give his soldiers a pep talk shortly before leading them into battle. According to Dio Cassius, not long before the sea battle of Actium commenced, Octavian gathered his followers and told them how he had given Antony every chance to do the right thing. But it was too late, as Cleopatra had already made him a slave to her will. "I did not think it right to treat Antony in the same way as Cleopatra," Octavian said.

> I hoped that he might, if not voluntarily, at least under pressure, decide to change his course in consequence of the [Roman] decrees that were passed against her. It was for these reasons that I did not declare war upon him at all. But he has treated all my efforts with contempt and disdain, and he refuses to be pardoned, although we offer him our pardon, or pitied, although we offer him our pity. He is either blind to reason or mad, for I have heard and can believe that he is bewitched by that accursed woman and therefore disregards all our efforts to show him goodwill and humanity. And so, being enslaved by her, he plunges into war, with all its attendant dangers, which he has accepted for her sake, against ourselves and against his country. What choice, then, remains to us, except our duty to oppose him, together with Cleopatra, and fight him off?

Quoted in Dio Cassius, *Roman History*, excerpted in *The Roman History: The Reign of Augustus,* trans. Ian Scott-Kilvert. New York: Penguin, 1987, p. 54.

edge against Octavian. Sure enough, in the spring of 32 BCE some of Rome's leading military generals left Italy and joined Antony and Cleopatra. So did almost three hundred senators, along with thousands of their supporters.

In fact, Octavian may well have lost the war had it not been for two key factors that worked in his favor. First, Cleopatra and Antony proved overconfident, which caused them to take too long to begin assembling their forces. As Plutarch pointed out, this overly casual attitude was one of their "greatest errors of judgment, since it gave Octavian the opportunity to complete his [military] preparations."[32]

The other important factor in Octavian's favor took the form of a person—his close associate Agrippa. Although he was only about thirty at the time, Agrippa was perceptive and resourceful, and he possessed plenty of battle experience. At Octavian's request, he took command of the 250 warships and 80,000 land fighters that Octavian then had at his disposal. Both men knew that Antony's and Cleopatra's forces were bigger—more than 500 warships and at least 100,000 soldiers. Yet Agrippa reasoned that his own vessels were more maneuverable and had more on-deck catapults than Antony's. Agrippa told Octavian that they must exploit those advantages. They should seize the initiative and push Antony into fighting at sea, Agrippa argued, and Octavian agreed.

Octavian and Agrippa swiftly led their forces to Greece, where Cleopatra and Antony were in the midst of still more public propaganda displays. The lovers' land troops and navy were not yet ready to fight, a fact that Agrippa took full advantage of. In March 31 BCE, he surprised and captured one of Antony's main naval bases, at Methone on Greece's southern coast. Meanwhile, following Agrippa's plan, Octavian marched his land forces to Actium, on Greece's western coast. These maneuvers cornered Cleopatra and Antony in southern Greece. Their only choices were to surrender or fight their way out of the trap.

> *"Octavian's ships resembled cavalry, now launching a charge, and now retreating . . . while Antony's were like heavy infantry, warding off the enemy's efforts to ram them, but also striving to hold them with their grappling-hooks."*[34]
>
> —The second-century Roman historian Dio Cassius.

The Beginning and the End

The second option—to fight—was the only one Antony and Cleopatra seriously considered. Another critical choice then arose—whether they should fight on land or at sea. Cleopatra argued for a sea battle, saying it was their best chance to escape the trap, and Antony, impressed by her natural strategic instincts, agreed.

The great battle, destined to shape Mediterranean history for generations to come, took place on September 2, 31 BCE, in the waters near Actium. Initially, the opposing fleets remained in place at a good distance from each other while the leaders on both sides tried to build up their fighters' morale. According to Plutarch, Antony visited many of his ships and "urged the soldiers to rely on the weight of their vessels," which were bigger than Octavian's. Antony told his men "to stand firm and fight exactly as if they were on land."[33] Meanwhile, Octavian told his own soldiers (as Dio recalled) that Antony was under the spell of a wicked quecn who had convinced him to turn traitor to his homeland. The twisted lovers must be defeated, Octavian warned, or that perverted woman might end up ruling Rome.

In the early afternoon, Antony ordered his ships to move forward and attack. Dio, who based his account on eyewitness reports, wrote that Agrippa's strategy was to form his own vessels into a huge crescent in an effort to surround Antony's forces. When the fleets met head-on, the ships commanded by Octavian and Agrippa used their

Octavian's fleet battles Antony and Cleopatra's forces in the waters near Actium in 31 BCE. When Cleopatra realized that she and Antony could not win, she retreated—and Antony followed, leaving behind most of his ships and men.

catapults to shoot large rocks at the opposing craft. Their swift ships also rammed several of Antony's and Cleopatra's slower vessels. In Dio's words, "Octavian's ships resembled cavalry, now launching a charge, and now retreating . . . while Antony's were like heavy infantry, warding off the enemy's efforts to ram them, but also striving to hold them with their grappling-hooks."[34]

When it became clear that the battle was steadily moving in Octavian's and Agrippa's favor, Cleopatra ordered the sixty ships in her squadron to retreat and escape the fray. Seeing her leaving, Antony followed, in the process abandoning most of his remaining ships and men. This may have been planned, in the event the fight went in the enemy's favor. Perhaps they reasoned that in such a case it was better to survive and thereby be able to fight and win later battles. What they could not then foresee was that such a scenario would not come to pass. Instead, Cleopatra and her Roman lover would soon face a sad truth. The immense bid for power they had so long anticipated had both begun and ended at Actium, and their days on earth were now numbered.

Chapter Five

Creating a Legend
for the Ages

Cleopatra and Antony were never able to recover from the disaster at Actium. They had lost some two hundred of their ships and more than five thousand sailors and soldiers. In theory, those precious resources could easily be replaced. But Antony and Cleopatra had run away in the midst of battle, leaving their followers to fend for themselves. Antony had also abandoned his land troops in southern Greece.

Partly for these reasons, many of the couple's former supporters now viewed them as having no chance of beating Octavian. Cleopatra and Antony learned of this new and stark reality firsthand when they tried "to make arrangements to carry on the war in Egypt both at sea and on land," in Dio Cassius's words. "For this purpose, they summoned all the neighboring tribes and rulers."[35] To the lovers' dismay, they found that most of their once large power base in the East had collapsed. Most leaders in the region now feared what Octavian might do to them if they continued to support Egypt's queen and her disgraced Roman partner.

Secret Negotiations and Nightly Parties

Antony and Cleopatra, who had fled back to Alexandria after escaping from Actium, now worried that the Ptolemaic kingdom and their children's legacy were in jeopardy. Unable to think of any other credible way out of their fix, they stooped to bribery. Cleopatra was still quite rich, after all. Perhaps, they hoped, Octavian could be bought off. They also appealed to him to show them mercy for sentimental reasons. According to Dio, they sent messengers to Octavian. The couriers carried "peace proposals for him and bribes of money for his supporters." Indeed, "Cleopatra promised to give him large sums of money, while Antony reminded him of their [former] friendship and their kinship by marriage."[36]

Octavian's immediate reactions to these proposals reveal how practical and calculating he was as a leader. Although his propaganda against Cleopatra had been harsh, privately he respected her intelligence and talents. He fully realized that she still had the resources to cause him trouble. Also, he worried that she might actually destroy much of her wealth before he could get his hands on it. So he sent her a secret message. According to Dio, that message said, "If she would kill Antony," Octavian "would grant her a pardon and leave her kingdom untouched." Octavian hoped that this approach would "dispose of Antony and keep Cleopatra and her treasure unharmed."[37]

> "If she would kill Antony, [Octavian] would grant her a pardon and leave her kingdom untouched."[37]
>
> —The second-century Roman historian Dio Cassius.

These secret negotiations stalled, however, when Cleopatra refused to slay Antony. Octavian had clearly miscalculated, not realizing that she actually deeply loved her Roman ally and had not been merely using him as a means to an end. She and Antony had no other choice now but to await Octavian's inevitable arrival in Egypt. At this dire moment, Cleopatra could have simply left her people to their own devices and concentrated on her own needs. Instead, she kept the government functioning and continued the day-to-day business of ruling.

In contrast, Antony seemed to lack his lover's fortitude and sense of duty. He reacted to their adverse situation by withdrawing from public life and wallowing in alcohol and depression. He was tortured by the reality that he had once stood near the pinnacle of Roman power. Yet he had betrayed his country and was now the object of humiliation and rejection. He attempted to kill himself more than once. But the handful of officers who remained loyal to him prevented him from taking his own life.

Eventually, Cleopatra persuaded Antony to join her in a series of nightly feasts and drinking parties in her palace. Together with some friends, they partied night after night. At times the celebrants talked about committing suicide together, as a group, when Octavian finally showed up. According to Plutarch, they called themselves the Order of the Inseparable Death.

Two Legendary Giants

The day of reckoning the revelers had unhappily anticipated came in July 30 BCE. Hearing that Octavian had landed an army on the coast near Alexandria, Antony donned his Roman uniform. Saying farewell to Cleopatra, he told her he was going to fulfill his duty to their cause

Cleopatra and Male Chauvinism

All reputable modern scholars now agree that much of Cleopatra's historical and cultural legacy has been shaped by the way that earlier male historians and writers portrayed her. More often than not, those portrayals were at least to some degree based on the mistaken notion that all women, even one as illustrious as Cleopatra, were intellectually inferior to men. Ohio State University scholar Duane W. Roller explains:

> Like all women, she suffers from male-dominated historiography [history writing] in both ancient and modern times and was often seen merely as an appendage of the men in her life or was stereotyped into typical chauvinistic female roles such as seductress or sorceress, one whose primary accomplishment was ruining the men she was involved with. In this view, she . . . played little role in the policy decisions of her own world. She was the only woman in classical antiquity to rule independently—not merely as a successor to a dead husband—and she desperately tried to salvage and keep alive a dying kingdom in the face of overwhelming Roman pressure. Descended from at least two companions of Alexander the Great, she had more stature than the Romans she opposed.

Duane W. Roller, *Cleopatra: A Biography.* New York: Oxford University Press, 2011, p. 2.

and rode out to do battle. He seems to have held out some small hope that his and Cleopatra's remaining ships and land troops might still do some damage to Octavian's forces. But the next morning that hope was crushed. The soldiers and sailors who had long followed Antony's and Cleopatra's orders abruptly acted in their own best interests and went over to Octavian's side.

Now completely alone, Antony rode back to the city, hoping to find and die with Cleopatra. He was horrified when he saw that Alexandria had fallen into chaos and heard someone say that the queen was dead. Realizing there was no longer anyone left to stop him from killing himself, he decided it was time to finish the job. As Plutarch told it, Antony went to his bed chamber, "stabbed himself with his own sword through the belly and fell upon the bed."[38]

> "Greetings, my lord, for now the gods have given supremacy to you and taken it from me."[39]
>
> —The second-century Roman historian Dio Cassius.

For reasons unknown, the wound Antony had inflicted on himself failed to kill him right away. A while later, as he slipped in and out of consciousness, one of Cleopatra's attendants arrived and carried him away to her still unfinished tomb. She had barricaded herself there, along with a majority of her gold, silver, and other valuables. The queen's servants lifted the stricken Antony up into the tomb, and a while later he died in her arms.

Not long after that, before Cleopatra could decide what to do next, Octavian's guards made their way into the tomb and captured her. He made sure she was treated well while she remained under house arrest in one section of the palace. A few days passed. Then these two legendary giants of the ancient world finally met face to face.

According to Dio, Cleopatra met the future first Roman emperor in a "superbly decorated apartment." She wore a magnificent dress, along with much glittering, priceless jewelry, and sat beside an array of "many different portraits and busts of Julius Caesar." In addition, she held in her lap "all the letters Caesar had sent her." As Octavian approached her, she stood up with her head held high and said in a pleasant tone, "Greetings, my lord, for now the gods have given supremacy to you and taken it from me."[39]

By all accounts, the two leaders got along well and showed no bitterness to each other. At some point she asked him if he would agree to bury her beside her beloved Antony, and Octavian promised he would do so. In the meantime, Octavian said, he planned to spare both her and her children. Clearly, he realized that if he killed her, much of her renowned treasure might remain forever hidden. Also, he planned to march her as a captive in his victory parade when he later returned to Rome.

After her ignoble defeat, Cloepatra meets with Octavian. Ancient texts say the two met in a beautifully decorated apartment surrounded by statues and portraits of Julius Caesar.

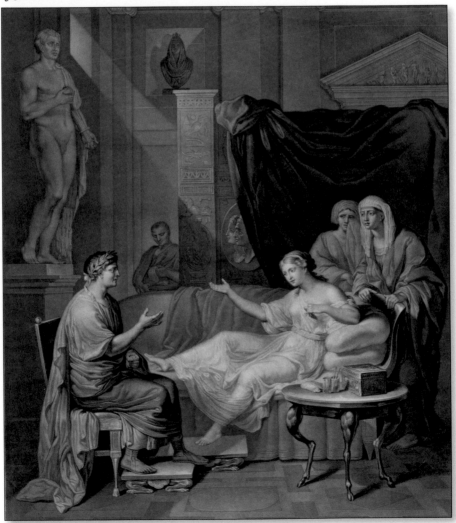

Cleopatra had already considered that such a humiliating fate awaited her in Rome, and she decided to rob her captor of that final victory. A day or two later, she locked herself in her tomb and took her life. The exact way she did it remains a mystery. One theory claims she pressed a poisonous snake called an asp to her chest, where it bit her.

Octavian's men find Cleopatra lying dead on a couch, dressed in her finest robes. In this illustration, the artist shows her dead serving women lying beside her. Although stories abound, how Cleopatra killed herself remains a mystery.

Other ancient accounts said she pricked her skin with a hairpin that had been dipped in potent poison.

In whatever manner she managed the deed, Octavian's men found her body lying "upon a golden couch dressed in her royal robes,"[40] in Plutarch's words. One of her servants knelt nearby, and a Roman soldier asked her, "Is this well done?" (By this, he meant, "Was this a well-thought-out plot to deceive Octavian?") The woman answered, "It is well done, and fitting for a princess descended of so many royal kings."[41]

An Extraordinary Legacy

When she chose to end her life on her own terms, Cleopatra was thirty-nine years old. For more than half her time on earth she had ruled Ptolemaic Egypt, showing herself to be equal in political talent, audacity, and courage to the three strongest men in her world—Caesar, Antony, and Octavian. In Dio's now famous words, "Through her own unaided genius she captivated the two greatest Romans of her time, and because of the third, she destroyed herself."[42]

Cleopatra could not destroy her extraordinary legacy, however. Its survival was due partly to the fact that Octavian made no attempt to suppress existing Roman and Greek accounts of her deeds, including her rebellion against Rome. (The administrative records of her reign were destroyed over the ensuing years, however.) Also, out of his genuine respect for her, he kept his promise to bury her alongside Antony. Octavian spared her and Antony's children as well; his sister Octavia raised and educated all three. Caesarion, Cleopatra's son by Caesar, did not fare as well. Worried that he might someday try to claim power in Caesar's name, Octavian had the boy quietly killed.

Cleopatra's persona lived on long after her death. The memory of her impressive accomplishments and forceful personality outlived Octavian and his descendants, as well as the last five centuries of

> *"Through her own unaided genius she captivated the two greatest Romans of her time, and because of the third, she destroyed herself."*[42]
>
> —The second-century Roman historian Dio Cassius.

An Agonizing Scene

When Cleopatra's servant carried Antony to her tomb, it was necessary to lift him up to a second-story window, since all of the other entrances had been blocked to keep Octavian's soldiers out. Plutarch later recorded the agonizing and touching scene, saying that Cleopatra

> showed herself at a window and let down cords and ropes to the ground. The slaves fastened Antony to these and the queen pulled him up with the help of her two waiting women, who were the only companions she had allowed to enter the monument with her. Those who were present say that there was never a more pitiable sight than the spectacle of Antony, covered with blood, struggling in his death agonies and stretching out his hands toward Cleopatra as he swung helplessly in the air. The task was almost beyond a woman's strength, and it was only with great difficulty that Cleopatra, clinging with both hands to the rope and with the muscles of her face distorted by the strain, was able to haul him up, while those on the ground encouraged her and shared her agony. When she had got him up and laid him upon a bed, she tore her dress and spread it over him, beat and lacerated her breasts, and smeared her face with the blood from his wounds. She called him her lord and husband and emperor and almost forgot her own misfortunes in her pity for his.

Plutarch, *Life of Antony,* in *Makers of Rome: Nine Lives by Plutarch,* trans. Ian Scott-Kilvert. New York: Penguin, 1965, pp. 341–42.

Roman civilization that followed. During the medieval era—the roughly thousand-year-long period that elapsed after Rome's fall in the late 400s CE—Cleopatra's true character and many of her specific deeds were no longer clear to most people. Yet she was still seen as a sort of mythical romantic figure and was well known for her love and loyalty to powerful men. One example appears in the writings of the renowned English poet Geoffrey Chaucer, author of the *Canter-*

bury Tales. He pictured her as part of a legendary literary and artistic tradition in which elegant noblewomen and dashing knights risked everything for love. Antony "had no fear of fighting or of dying to keep her safe," Chaucer wrote. "And she, the queen, in turn adored this knight, for his great worth and for his chivalry."[43]

Such highly romanticized images of Cleopatra also frequently made it into late medieval and early modern art. In 1534, for instance, the great Italian painter Michelangelo painted her with serpents in her hair. This was a reference to the popular tale in which she died of an asp's poisonous bite.

Stage Plays and Films

In these same years, Cleopatra began to appear as a character in European stage plays. The best-known example remains English dramatist William Shakespeare's *Antony and Cleopatra*, first performed in 1607. Shakespeare based his version primarily on Plutarch's biography of Antony. In Shakespeare's powerful, at times heart-rending tragedy, Cleopatra is portrayed as a flawed yet ultimately noble character. It is still regularly performed today, and in 1972 actor Charlton Heston directed and starred in a colorful film version of the story.

Of the many modern stage shows written about Cleopatra, one of the most popular is still *Caesar and Cleopatra*, written in 1898 by another great English playwright, George Bernard Shaw. This version of the exploits of the famous Greek queen of Egypt is more light-hearted and humorous than most others. Shaw envisioned Cleopatra as initially a mixed-up young woman who is afraid of the Romans. As the story progresses, however, she learns about life and politics from the older, wiser Caesar. Shaw's play became a film in 1946, with Vivien Leigh (who played Scarlet O'Hara in *Gone with the Wind*) as Cleopatra.

Many other movies were made about Cleopatra in the twentieth century. These productions brought her legendary character and story to millions of people who had never read the literary versions by Plutarch, Shakespeare, Shaw, and others. There were at least six silent films made about Cleopatra before 1930. The first major sound version was director

Cecil B. DeMille's 1934 spectacle, *Cleopatra*, with Claudette Colbert in the title role. Several other actresses played the ancient queen in the decades that followed. But far and away the most expensive and celebrated movie about her was the 1963 blockbuster that starred Elizabeth Taylor

Elizabeth Taylor plays the young and beautiful Egyptian queen in the 1963 movie, **Cleopatra.** *Books, plays, and movies have kept alive the larger-than-life legend and personality of Egypt's last pharaoh.*

as Cleopatra, Richard Burton as Antony, Rex Harrison as Caesar, and Roddy McDowall as Octavian.

An Endlessly Fascinating Woman

Cleopatra will surely continue to inspire more plays, films, and paintings. New history books that try to summarize or explore her compelling personality, life, and legend are also likely to emerge. Probably no single artistic or literary work will ever capture Cleopatra in her mystifying entirety. As biographer Joann Fletcher aptly puts it, "it is always a struggle to root out the real personality" of a famous and influential historical figure. This is true, Fletcher adds,

> especially in the case of Cleopatra, who even in her own lifetime was many different things to many different people. This determined leader, brilliant politician, erudite scholar, and mother of four was a multifaceted character who could really be all things to all people. To the Romans she was a deluded and drunken whore, to the Greeks and Middle Eastern peoples a beneficent and glorious liberator, to the Egyptians their living goddess and monarch, and in her own mind, Alexander's true successor. And in amongst the spin and propaganda from so many diverse sources, attempts to reach the woman herself have proved challenging to say the least. Ultimately, only a saga covering several millennia, three continents, and a whole range of diverse evidence could ever hope to make sense of this incredibly complex yet endlessly fascinating woman.[44]

Source Notes

Introduction: Searching for the Real Cleopatra

1. Quoted in Dio Cassius, *Roman History*, excerpted in *The Roman History: The Reign of Augustus*, trans. Ian Scott-Kilvert. New York: Penguin, 1987, pp. 52–53.

2. Quoted in Dio Cassius, *Roman History*, p. 53.

3. Horace, *Cleopatra*, trans. Barklie Henry, in *The Latin Poets*, ed. Francis R.B. Godolphin. New York: Random House, 1949, p. 343.

4. Lucy Hughes-Hallett, *Cleopatra: Histories, Dreams and Distortions*. New York: HarperCollins, 1991, p. 1.

5. Stacy Schiff, *Cleopatra: A Life*. Boston: Back Bay, 2011, p. 2.

Chapter One: Growing Up in Rome's Shadow

6. Zahi Hawass, *Cleopatra: The Search for the Last Queen of Egypt*. Washington, DC: National Geographic, 2010, p. 12.

7. Joann Fletcher, *Cleopatra the Great: The Woman Behind the Legend*. New York: HarperCollins, 2008, p. 2.

8. Naphtali Lewis, *Greeks in Ptolemaic Egypt*. Oxford: Clarendon, 1986, p. 154.

9. Hawass, *Cleopatra*, p. 17.

10. Hawass, *Cleopatra*, pp. 17–19.

11. Schiff, *Cleopatra*, p. 29.

Chapter Two: Securing Powerful Allies

12. Julius Caesar, *The Alexandrian War*, in *Caesar: The Civil War*, trans. John Carter. New York: Oxford University Press, 1997, p. 133.

13. Caesar, *The Alexandrian War*, p. 135.

14. Plutarch, *Life of Caesar*, in *Fall of the Roman Republic: Six Lives by Plutarch*, trans. Rex Warner. New York: Penguin, 1972, p. 290.

15. Plutarch, *Life of Caesar*, p. 290.

16. Plutarch, *Life of Caesar*, p. 290.

17. Schiff, *Cleopatra*, p. 126.

18. Plutarch, *Life of Antony*, in *Makers of Rome: Nine Lives by Plutarch*, trans. Ian Scott-Kilvert. New York: Penguin, 1965, p. 294.

19. Plutarch, *Life of Antony*, p. 294.

Chapter Three: Proving Herself an Effective Ruler

20. Seneca, *Natural Questions*, vol. 2, trans. T.H. Corcoran. Cambridge, MA: Harvard University Press, 1972, p. 33.

21. Philo of Alexandria, *Embassy to Gaius*, trans. F.H. Colson. Cambridge, MA: Harvard University Press, 1962, p. 129.

22. Quoted in Athenaeus, *Sophists at Dinner*, vol. 4, trans. Charles B. Gulick. Cambridge, MA: Harvard University Press, 1928, p. 147.

23. Hughes-Hallett, *Cleopatra*, pp. 75–76.

24. Plutarch, *Life of Antony*, p. 322.

25. Diana Preston, *Cleopatra and Antony: Power, Love, and Politics in the Ancient World*. New York: Walker, 2009, p. 75.

26. Ernle Bradford, *Cleopatra*. New York: Harcourt, Brace, Jovanovich, 1972, p. 12.

Chapter Four: Challenging the Might of Rome

27. Plutarch, *Life of Antony*, p. 326.

28. Dio Cassius, *Roman History*, pp. 38–39.

29. Plutarch, *Life of Antony*, p. 321.

30. Plutarch, *Life of Antony*, p. 322.

31. Dio Cassius, *Roman History*, p. 38.

32. Plutarch, *Life of Antony*, p. 324.

33. Plutarch, *Life of Antony*, p. 330.

34. Dio Cassius, *Roman History*, p. 59.

Chapter Five: Creating a Legend for the Ages

35. Dio Cassius, *Roman History*, pp. 67–68.

36. Dio Cassius, *Roman History*, pp. 68–69.

37. Dio Cassius, *Roman History*, p. 70.

38. Plutarch, *Life of Antony*, p. 341.

39. Quoted in Dio Cassius, *Roman History*, p. 73.

40. Plutarch, *Life of Antony*, p. 347.

41. Quoted in Plutarch, *Life of Antony*, p. 347.

42. Dio Cassius, *Roman History*, p. 76.

43. Geoffrey Chaucer, "The Legend of Cleopatra," in *The Legend of Good Women*, trans. Ann McMillan. Houston: Rice University Press, 1987, pp. 83–86.

44. Fletcher, *Cleopatra the Great*, p. 7.

Important Events in the Life of Cleopatra

BCE

305

Ptolemy, an officer serving under Alexander the Great, declares himself ruler of Egypt; his action marks the start of the Ptolemaic dynasty— which will include Cleopatra.

100

Birth of Julius Caesar, a Roman who will later become ruler of the Mediterranean world, as well as Cleopatra's ally and lover.

circa 83

Birth of Marcus Antonius (Mark Antony), the Roman military officer who will later become Cleopatra's ally and lover after Caesar's death.

80

Cleopatra's father, Ptolemy XII Auletes, becomes Egypt's king.

69

Birth of Cleopatra, daughter of Auletes and future last pharaoh of Egypt.

63

Birth of Octavius Caesar (Octavian), later Caesar's adopted son, Cleopatra's nemesis, and, under the name Augustus, the first Roman emperor.

51

Auletes dies, leaving his throne to Cleopatra and her younger brother, Ptolemy XIII.

49

Young Ptolemy and his adult regent force Cleopatra into exile.

48

Caesar arrives in Egypt and forms an alliance with Cleopatra, who has just returned from exile.

47

Caesar defeats Ptolemy and his supporters and places Cleopatra on the Egyptian throne.

44

Cleopatra visits Rome, where, on March 15, Caesar is assassinated by a group of Roman senators.

43

Antony, Octavian, and a powerful general named Lepidus form a strong political alliance.

41

Antony summons Cleopatra to his headquarters at Tarsus in Anatolia, and the two become allies.

40

Cleopatra gives birth to twins, fathered by Antony.

34

Planning to challenge Octavian for control of the Roman world, Cleopatra and Antony stage the Donations of Alexandria, a huge ceremony that proclaims their power.

31

Octavian defeats Antony and Cleopatra at Actium in western Greece.

30

Antony and Cleopatra commit suicide, and Octavian annexes Egypt as a Roman province.

For Further Research

Books

Charles River Publishers, *Caesar and Cleopatra: History's Most Powerful Couple*. Charleston, SC: CreateSpace, 2013.

Zahi Hawass, *Cleopatra: The Search for the Last Queen of Egypt*. Washington, DC: National Geographic, 2010.

Barbara Kramer, *Cleopatra*. Washington, DC: National Geographic Children's, 2015.

Duane W. Roller, *Cleopatra: A Biography*. New York: Oxford University Press, 2011.

Stacy Schiff, *Cleopatra: A Life*. Boston: Back Bay, 2011.

Vicky A. Shecter, *Cleopatra Rules! The Amazing Life of the Original Teen Queen*. Honesdale, PA: Boyds Mills, 2013.

Websites

Actium (31 BCE), Livus.org (www.livius.org/battle/actium-31-bce). The great battle in which Cleopatra's fortunes collapsed is explained here in detail as part of the excellent online ancient history website maintained by noted Dutch historian Jona Lendering.

Ancient Egypt Film Site (www.ancientegyptfilmsite.nl). This fascinating site tells about the various movies made about Cleopatra and her exploits over the years.

Ancient Egypt Online (www.ancientegyptonline.co.uk). Researcher Jenny Hill provides a wealth of information on ancient Egypt, including an examination of Cleopatra's character and a synopsis of her relationship with Julius Caesar.

Ancient Egypt Site (www.ancient-egypt.org). This site, a sturdy overview of ancient Egyptian history and culture, provides some useful background material for better understanding what the world was like in Cleopatra's time.

Mark Antony, History.com (www.history.com/topics/ancient-history/mark-antony). A brief overview of the Roman notable with whom Cleopatra had children and formed an alliance to challenge Rome.

Ptolemies, Livius.org (www.livius.org/dynasty/ptolemies). Historian Jona Lendering provides information about the Greek dynasty of which Cleopatra was the last member.

The Search for Cleopatra, National Geographic (http://ngm.nationalgeographic.com/2011/07/cleopatra/brown-text). This section by Chip Brown seeks to disentangle the real Cleopatra from the mass of fiction written about her over the ages.

Timeline of the Life of Cleopatra, San Jose State University (www.sjsu.edu/faculty/watkins/cleopatra.htm). A detailed chronological look at Cleopatra's life and achievements.

Was Cleopatra Beautiful? Encyclopedia Roma (http://penelope.uchicago.edu/~grout/encyclopaedia_romana/miscellanea/cleopatra/bust.html). Researcher James Grout cites Plutarch, Dio Cassius, and other ancient historians in an effort to piece together a visual image of Cleopatra.

Index

Picture Credits

About the Author

Historian and award-winning author Don Nardo has written numerous books about the ancient world, its peoples, and their cultures, including volumes on the Babylonians, Assyrians, Persians, Minoans, Greeks, Etruscans, Romans, and others. He is also the author of single-volume encyclopedias on ancient Mesopotamia, ancient Greece, ancient Rome, and Greek and Roman mythology. In addition, Nardo composes and arranges orchestral music. He lives with his wife, Christine, in Massachusetts.